THE HOLY ROSARY

With a Brief Guide for
Contemplating the Twenty Mysteries

Rev. Fr. John C. Portavella

Leonine Publishers
Phoenix, Arizona

Copyright © 2018 Rev. Fr. John C. Portavella, J.C.D.

E-mail: *frjohn.portavella@gmail.com*

(With ecclesiastical approval)

All rights reserved. No part of this book may be reproduced or transmitted in any form or by any means, electronic or mechanical, including photocopying, recording, or by any information storage or retrieval system now existing or to be invented, without written permission from the respective copyright holder(s), except for the inclusion of brief quotations in a review.

Published by
Leonine Publishers LLC
Phoenix, Arizona, USA

ISBN-13: 978-1-942190-44-8

Library of Congress Control Number: 2018937956

10 9 8 7 6 5 4 3 2 1

Visit us online at www.leoninepublishers.com
For more information: info@leoninepublishers.com

The Our Father

V. Our Father, who art in heaven, hallowed be thy name; thy kingdom come; thy will be done on earth as it is in heaven.

R. Give us this day our daily bread; and forgive us our trespasses as we forgive those who trespass against us; and lead us not into temptation, but deliver us from evil. Amen.

The Hail Mary

V. Hail Mary, full of grace, the Lord is with thee; blessed art thou among women, and blessed is the fruit of thy womb, Jesus.

R. Holy Mary, Mother of God, pray for us sinners, now and at the hour of our death. Amen.

The Glory Be

V. Glory be to the Father, and to the Son, and to the Holy Spirit.

R. As it was in the beginning, is now, and ever shall be, world without end. Amen.

Visit to the Blessed Sacrament

Recite three sets:
>Our Father...
>Hail Mary...
>Glory be...

Recite a Spiritual Communion:
>I wish, Lord, to receive you with the purity, humility, and devotion with which your most Holy Mother received you, with the spirit and fervor of the saints.

Make the Sign of the Cross:
>In the name of the Father, and of the Son, and of the Holy Spirit. Amen.

Recite the Apostles' Creed:
>I believe in God, the Father almighty, creator of heaven and earth; and in Jesus Christ, His only Son, Our Lord; who was conceived by the Holy Spirit, born of the Virgin Mary, suffered under Pontius Pilate, was crucified, died, and was buried. He descended into hell: the third day He arose again from the dead into heaven, sits at the right hand of God, the

Father almighty; from thence He shall come to judge the living and the dead. I believe in the Holy Spirit, the Holy Catholic Church, the communion of saints, the forgiveness of sins, the resurrection of the body, and life everlasting. Amen.

Then:

One Our Father...
Three Hail Marys...
One Glory be...

Start each decade by announcing the Mystery and meditating upon it for a few seconds. At the end of every decade, you may recite the following Fatima prayer:

O Jesus, forgive us our sins, save us from the fire of hell, bring all souls to heaven, especially those who are in more need of your mercy.

Joyful Mysteries

(Monday / Saturday)

1ˢᵗ

The Annunciation

"And the angel said to her, the Holy Spirit will come upon you, and the power of the Most High will overshadow you..." And Mary said, "Behold, I am the handmaid of the Lord; let it be done according to your word." *(Lk 1:35, 38)*

"At the enchantment of this virginal phrase, the Word was made flesh."
(St. Josemaría Escrivá, Holy Rosary)

Resolution:

I will put all my heart into living my Christian vocation.

2ND

The Visitation

"Blessed are you among women, and blessed is the fruit of your womb! And why is this granted to me, that the mother of my Lord should come to me? For behold, when the voice of your greeting came to my ears, the babe in my womb leapt for joy." *(Lk 1:42-44)*

"Mary brought joy to her cousin's home, because she brought Christ."
(St. Josemaría Escrivá, Furrow, 566)

Resolution:

I will go out of my way to share my faith and my joy with others.

3ʀᴅ

The Birth of Jesus

"And while they were there the time came for her to be delivered. And she gave birth to her first-born son and wrapped him with swaddling clothes and laid him in a manger."
(Lk 2:6-7)

"Jesus Christ, God and Man. It is one of the mighty works of God which we should reflect upon and to be thankful for. He has come to bring peace on earth to men of good will."
(St. Josemaría Escrivá, Christ is Passing By, 13)

Resolution:

I will be satisfied with what God has given me, and I will not compare myself with anyone.

4th

The Presentation

"And when the time came for her purification according to the law of Moses, they brought him up to Jerusalem to present him to the Lord." *(Lk 2:22)*

"Purification! You and I certainly do need purification. Atonement and more than atonement, Love."
(St. Josemaría Escrivá, Holy Rosary, 4th Joyful Mystery)

Resolution:

I will dedicate myself to the service of God and others.

5ᵗʰ

The Finding of Jesus in the Temple

"After three days they found him in the temple, sitting among teachers, listening to them and asking them questions… And his mother said to him, Son, why have you treated us so?… And he said to them, How is it that you sought me?"
(Lk 2:46, 48, 49)

"The Mother of God who sought keenly her Son, lost without her fault, will help us to rectify when due to our frivolity or sins we may not manage to spot Christ."
(St. Josemaría Escrivá, Friends of God, 278)

Resolution:

I will avoid excessive attachment to my work or to my family, in order to have time for God.

Luminous Mysteries

(Thursday)

1ˢᵗ

Jesus' Baptism in the Jordan

"And when Jesus was baptized, He went up immediately from the water, and behold the heavens were opened and He saw the spirit of God descending like a dove, and alighting on Him and lo, a voice from heaven, saying. 'This is my beloved Son, with whom I am well pleased.'" *(Mt 3:16-17)*

"Christ descends into the waters, the innocent One who became 'sin' for our sake, the heavens open wide and the voice of the Father declares Him the beloved Son, while the Spirit descends on Him to invest Him with the mission that He is to carry out."
(Pope St. John Paul II, Rosarium Virginis Mariae, 21)

Resolution:

I will try hard to please God my Father in all I do.

2ND

Jesus' Self-manifestation at the Wedding of Cana

"This, the first of His signs, Jesus did at Cana in Galilee, and manifested His glory and His disciples believed in Him." *(Jn 2:11)*

"Christ changes water into wine and opens the hearts of the disciples to faith, thanks to the intervention of Mary, the first among the believers."

(Pope St. John Paul II, Rosarium Virginis Mariae, 21)

"Mary, teacher of prayer. See how she asks her Son at Cana. And how she insists, confidently, perseveringly... And how she succeeds."

(St. Josemaría Escrivá, The Way, 502)

Resolution:

I will seek the intercession of Our Lady to obtain all I need.

3ʳᵈ

Jesus' Proclamation of the Kingdom of God, with His Call to Conversion

"Jesus came into Galilee, preaching the gospel of God and saying, 'The time is fulfilled, and the kingdom of God is at hand; repent, and believe in the gospel.'" *(Mk 1:14-15)*

Jesus "forgives the sins of all who draw near to Him in humble trust." He proclaims "the inauguration of that ministry of mercy which He continues to exercise until the end of the world, particularly through the Sacrament of Reconciliation, which He has entrusted to His Church."
(Pope St. John Paul II, Rosarium Virginis Mariae, 21)

Resolution:

I will be once more converted by means of the contrite reception of the Sacrament of Penance.

4TH

Jesus' Transfiguration

"He took with Him Peter and John and James, and went up on the mountain to pray. And as He was praying, the appearance of His countenance was altered and His raiment became dazzling white." *(Lk 9:28-29)*

"On mount Tabor the glory of the Godhead shines forth from the face of Christ as the Father commands the astonished Apostles to 'listen to Him.'" He is preparing them for the agony of the Passion, and strengthening them to continue with Him to the joy of the resurrection and to a life transfigured by the Holy Spirit.
(Pope St. John Paul II, Rosarium Virginis Mariae, 21)

Resolution:

I will listen to Christ and be more attentive to my spiritual formation.

5ᵗʰ

The Institution of the Eucharist

"And He said to them; I have earnestly desired to eat this Passover with you before I suffer... And He took bread, and when He had given thanks He broke it and gave it to them, saying, 'This is my body which is given up for you. Do this in memory of me.'" *(Lk 22:15, 19)*

"Christ offers His body and blood as spiritual food under the signs of bread and wine, and testifies 'to the end' His love for humanity, for whose salvation He will offer Himself in sacrifice."
(Pope St. John Paul II, Rosarium Virginis Mariae, 21)

"What we cannot do, our Lord can. Jesus Christ, perfect God and perfect Man, does not leave a symbol, but a reality. He Himself stays."
(St. Josemaría Escrivá, Christ is Passing By, 83)

Resolution:

I will say a spiritual communion when passing near a place where Jesus is kept in the tabernacle.

Sorrowful Mysteries

(Tuesday / Friday)

1ˢᵗ

The Agony in the Garden

"And He knelt, and prayed saying: 'Father if thou are willing, remove this cup from me; nevertheless, not my will, but thine be done.' And there appeared to Him an angel from heaven, strengthening Him." *(Lk 22:41-43)*

"Pain has a place in God's plans."
(St. Josemaría Escrivá, Christ is Passing By, 168)

Resolution:

I will be patient with others and with myself.

2ᴺᴰ

The Scourging at the Pillar

"Then Pilate took Jesus and had Him scourged."
(Jn 19:1)

"Bound to the pillar. Covered with wounds. The blows of the lash sound upon His torn flesh, upon His undefiled flesh... Look at Him...slowly. After this can you ever fear penance?"

(St. Josemaría Escrivá, Holy Rosary, Sorrowful Mysteries, 2)

Resolution:

I will not complain!

3ʳᵈ

The Crowning with Thorns

"And the soldiers plaited a crown of thorns, and put it on His head, and arrayed Him in a purple robe, they came up to Him saying, 'Hail, King of the Jews!' And struck Him with their hands." *(Jn 19:2-3)*

"You and I... haven't we crowned Him anew with thorns and struck Him and spat on Him?"
(St. Josemaría Escrivá, Holy Rosary, Sorrowful Mysteries, 3)

Resolution:

I will not entertain grudges or impure thoughts in my mind.

4ᵀᴴ

Jesus Carries His Cross

"So they took Jesus, and He went out, bearing His own cross, to the place called in Hebrew, Golgotha." *(Jn 19:17)*

"If anyone would follow me… we are sad living the Passion of our Lord Jesus. See how lovingly He embraces the Cross. Learn from Him. Jesus carries the Cross for you: you carry it for Jesus."

*(St. Josemaría Escrivá, Holy Rosary,
Sorrowful Mysteries, 4)*

Resolution:

I will take every contradiction as a caress of our Lord and as an opportunity to co-redeem with Him.

5TH

The Crucifixion

"He said to His Mother, 'Woman, behold your son.' Then He said to the disciple, 'Behold your Mother.' And from this hour the disciple took her into his home." *(Jn 19:26-27)*

"Say to her: Mother of mine–yours because you are hers on many counts–may your love bind me to your Son's cross; may I not lack the faith, nor the courage, nor the daring, to carry out the will of our Jesus."

(St. Josemaría Escrivá, The Way, 497)

Resolution:

I will not center my life on myself, but on Jesus Christ and on others for His sake.

Glorious Mysteries

(Wednesday / Sunday)

1ST

The Resurrection

"Peter therefore went out, and the other disciple, and they went to the tomb... Simon Peter came following him, and he went into the tomb, and saw the linen cloths lying there... Then the other disciple also went in, who had come first to the tomb, and he saw and believed." *(Jn 20:3, 6, 8)*

"Christ is alive. This is the great truth which fills our faith with meaning. Jesus who died on the cross, has risen... This is the day which the Lord has made; let us rejoice and be glad on it."
(St. Josemaría Escrivá, Christ is Passing By, 102)

Resolution:

I will not postpone bringing my friends closer to Jesus, the living Lord.

2ᴺᴰ

The Ascension

"Now He led them out toward Bethany, and He lifted up His hands and blessed them. And it came to pass as He blessed them, that He parted from them and was carried up into heaven. And they worshiped Him, and returned to Jerusalem with great joy."

(Lk 24:50-52)

"Christ awaits us. We are 'citizens of heaven,' and at the same time fully-fledged citizens of this earth (...) Let us be contemplative souls, carrying on an unceasing dialogue with our Lord at all hours."

(St. Josemaría Escrivá, Christ is Passing By, 126)

Resolution:

I will not speak badly of anyone, and I will dissuade others from backbiting.

3ʳᵈ

The Descent of the Holy Spirit

"And when the days of Pentecost were drawing to a close, they were all together in one place… And there appeared to them parted tongues as of fire… And they were all filled with the Holy Spirit and began to speak in foreign tongues, even as the Holy Spirit prompted them to speak." *(Acts 2:1, 3-4)*

"Then Peter stood up with the eleven and addressed the people in a loud voice. We people from a hundred nations, hear him. Each of us hears him in his own language."
(St. Josemaría Escrivá, Holy Rosary, Glorious Mysteries, 1)

Resolution:

With the help of the Holy Spirit, I will do more personal apostolate work.

4ᵀᴴ

The Assumption

"You are all fair, my love; there is no flaw in you... Who is this who looks forth as the dawn, fair as the moon, bright as the sun?"
(Song of Solomon 4:7, 6:10)

"God has taken Mary, body and soul, to heaven, and the angels rejoice... The most blessed Trinity receives and showers honors on the Daughter, Mother and Spouse of God."
(St. Josemaría Escrivá, Holy Rosary, Glorious Mysteries, 4)

Resolution:

I will live a pure life, guarding especially my sight and my thoughts.

5ᵀᴴ

The Coronation of the Blessed Virgin

"A great sign appeared in heaven: a woman clothed with the sun, and the moon was under her feet, and upon her head a crown of twelve stars." *(Rev 12:1)*

"It is indeed just that the Father, the Son, and the Holy Spirit should crown the Blessed Virgin as Queen and Lady of all created things. You have to make use of her power. With the daring of a child, join in this celebration in Heaven (....) She is expecting something from you too." *(St. Josemaría Escrivá, The Forge, 285)*

Resolution:

I will pray the Holy Rosary every day, even if I feel tired.

After the Rosary you may recite:

Hail, Holy Queen, mother of mercy, hail our life our sweetness and our hope! To thee do we cry, poor banished children of Eve; to thee we send up our sighs, mourning and weeping in this vale of tears. Turn, then, most gracious advocate, thine eyes of mercy towards us, and after this our exile, show unto us the blessed fruit of thy womb, Jesus, O clement, O loving, O sweet Virgin Mary!

V. Pray for us, O Holy Mother of God.

R. That we may be made worthy of the promises of Christ.

Let us pray. O God whose only begotten Son, by His life death and resurrection, has purchased for us the rewards of eternal life, grant we beseech thee, that by meditating upon the mysteries of the most Holy Rosary of the Blessed Virgin Mary, we may imitate what they contain and obtain what they promise. Through Christ our Lord.

R. Amen.

Litany of the Blessed Virgin

Lord, have mercy on us.
Christ, have mercy on us.

Lord, have mercy on us. Christ, hear us.
Christ, graciously hear us.

God the Father of heaven,
Have mercy on us.

God the Son, redeemer of the world,
Have mercy on us.

God the Holy Spirit,
Have mercy on us.

Holy Trinity one God,
Have mercy on us.

Holy Mary,
Pray for us.
(repeat this response after every phrase)

Holy Mother of God,
Holy Virgin of virgins,
Mother of Christ,
Mother of the Church,
Mother of divine grace,
Mother most pure,

Mother most chaste,
Mother inviolate,
Mother undefiled,
Mother most amiable,
Mother most admirable,
Mother of good counsel,
Mother of our Creator,
Mother of our Savior,
Virgin most prudent,
Virgin most venerable,
Virgin most renowned,
Virgin most powerful,
Virgin most merciful,
Virgin most faithful,
Mirror of justice,
Seat of wisdom,
Cause of our joy,
Spiritual vessel,
Vessel of honor,
Singular vessel of devotion,
Mystical rose,
Tower of David,
Tower of ivory,
House of gold,
Ark of the covenant,
Gate of heaven,
Morning Star,
Health of the sick,
Refuge of sinners,
Comforter of the afflicted,
Help of Christians,
Queen of angels,
Queen of patriarchs,
Queen of prophets,
Queen of apostles,
Queen of martyrs,
Queen of confessors,
Queen of virgins,
Queen of all saints,
Queen conceived without original sin,
Queen assumed into heaven,
Queen of the most Holy Rosary,
Queen of the family,
Queen of peace,

V. Lamb of God, who takes away the sins of the world,
R. *Spare us, O Lord.*

V. Lamb of God, who takes away the sins of the world,
R. *Graciously hear us.*

V. Lamb of God, who takes away the sins of the world,
R. *Have mercy on us.*

V. Pray for us, O Holy Mother of God,
R. *That we may be made worthy of the promises of Christ.*

For the needs of the Church and the State.
   Our Father... Hail Mary... Glory be...

For the (arch)bishop of this diocese and his intentions.
   Our Father... Hail Mary... Glory be...

For the holy souls in Purgatory.
   Our Father... Hail Mary... Glory be...
   May they rest in peace. Amen.

About Leonine Publishers

Leonine Publishers LLC makes fine Catholic literature available to Catholics throughout the English-speaking world. Leonine Publishers offers an innovative "hybrid" approach to book publication that helps authors as well as readers. Please visit our web site at www.leoninepublishers.com to learn more about us. Browse our online bookstore to find more solid Catholic titles to uplift, challenge, and inspire.

Our patron and namesake is Pope Leo XIII, a prudent, yet uncompromising pope during the stormy years at the close of the 19th century. Please join us as we ask his intercession for our family of readers and authors.

Do you have a book inside you? Visit our web site today. Leonine Publishers accepts manuscripts from Catholic authors like you. If your book is selected for publication, you will have an active part in the production process. This book is an example of our growing selection of literature for the busy Catholic reader of the 21st century.

www.leoninepublishers.com

About the Author

Father John C. Portavella holds a master's degree in Chemistry from the University of Barcelona and a doctorate in Canon Law from the University of Santo Tomas (Angelicum) in Rome. He was ordained a priest for the Opus Dei prelature and has served in the USA and in the Philippines.

He is the author of *Planning the Journey of Life* (Leonine Publishers), *Why God Hides* (Sophia Institute Press) and *Means to Live a Happy and Chaste Life* (Leonine Publishers).

www.ingramcontent.com/pod-product-compliance
Lightning Source LLC
Chambersburg PA
CBHW041811040426
42450CB00001B/1